For Brian and Carolyn and your trusty companions,
Bertie and Worcester.

First Published in the UK 2024
Copyright © Leah Amir 2024
All rights reserved

ISBN: 9798320072159

Dusty
the dog

by Leah
Amir

Dusty the dog is feeling rather surplus.
With his owner gone he's lost his purpose.

Now he's *nervous* and all **alone**,
siting in the corner of a dog home.

Everyday people come by and stare,
"What a sad looking dog" **they all declare.**

He's not yet been chosen as a pet.
This has made Dusty quite upset.

With his *scraggly* grey and mottled fur,
it's other dogs that people prefer.

Maybe today, will be the day;
someone will come by, take him away.

Down the road is little Daisy;
she's super excited, going *crazy*.

Today her loneliness is going to end,
today she's going to find a new friend .

She's taking a trip with her mum and dad,
to help her feel just a little less sad.

The dog shelter is warm, and very inviting.
Daisy finds everything new and exciting.

They walk along the kennels, row by row;
whistling, smiling and saying *"hello"*.

But who to choose, it's such a hard choice.

Some are quiet,

others show their voice.

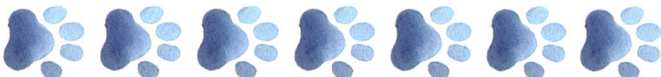

Dusty lies, with his head hung low.
He doesn't feel like putting on a **show.**

Still **and** *silent* **he stays all day,
undisturbed in every way.**

But in the distance he hears a squeal.
An unfamiliar noise, he's not sure how to feel.

Daisy's full of excitement and frill,
so Dusty stays low, and very still.

Walking past each silver cage,
she sees how all the dogs behave.

Some are lively, jumping all around,
their paws barely touching the ground.

Daisy dismisses the dogs one by one,
trying to imagine where each one is from.

Until she spots one *sad* looking dog;
pointing through the bars, she gives a nod.

"He's the one I want to take home,
we'll be best friends, never alone".

Dusty notices her twinkling toes.
He turns, and picks up his gloomy nose.

They gaze at each other, very **deeply**;
understanding one another, *utterly*, completely.

Dusty stands in front of Daisy;
no longer looking sad and rather lazy.

His ears twitching and tail swaying,
"Please can I have him" **Daisy is saying.**

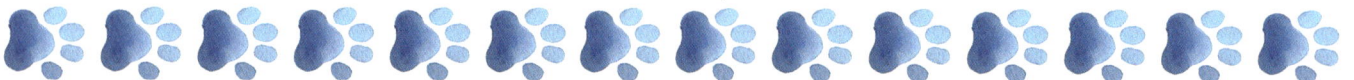

"Perfect, of course", the attendant declares,
"Let's do the paperwork, tie up the affairs".

They sign the forms, and pay the cash.
Then Dusty is theirs as quick as a flash.

In the car, they're on their way,
to start a friendship, full of play.

Leaping, *running* and doing tricks,
playing with balls and catching sticks.

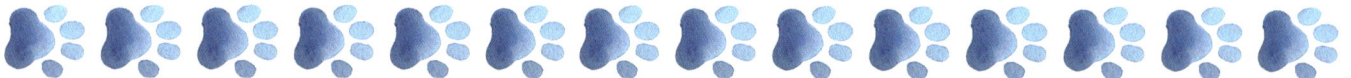

Daisy and Dusty are full of joy.
One happy girl and one happy boy.

No longer *sad*, *lost* and *alone*,
as a pair they've grown and grown.

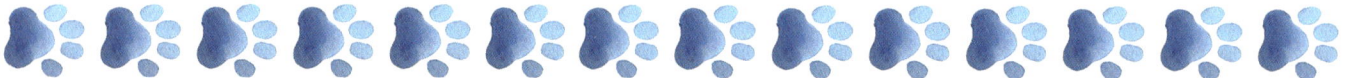

To find the right one can take a while;
but when you know, it will make you smile.

A friendship that will never end.
Someone on whom you can truly **depend**.

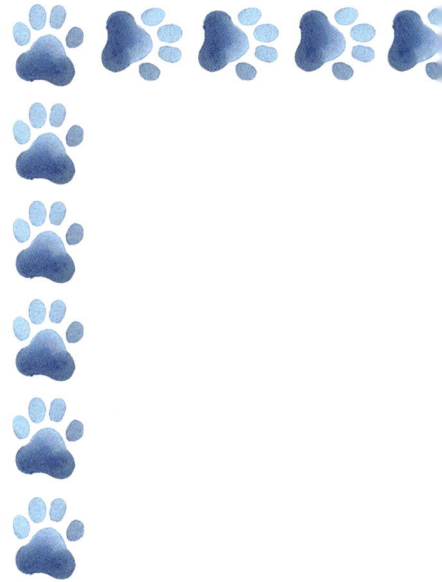

Printed in Great Britain
by Amazon

39577429R00025